THE FOUR BLUE WALLS

The Four Blue Walls

AMARA KURSHA

Duluth, Ga

The Four Blue Walls
Copyright © 2020 Amara Kursha

All rights reserved.

No part of this book may be reproduced or transmitted in any form or by any means, electronic or mechanical, including photocopying, recording or by any information storage and retrieval system, without written permission from the publisher, except for the inclusion of brief quotations in a review.

Address inquiries to the publisher

The Word Herd
P.O. Box 956324
Duluth, GA 30095

Learn more about the author at
www.thewordherd.com

ISBN 978-0-9990909-2-3 (print)
ISBN 978-0-9990909-3-0 (ebook)

Library of Congress Control Number: 2020915629

Edited and composed by Annette Johnson, Allwrite Communications Inc.

Printed in the United States of America

DEDICATION

One Time for the 4-6-2-9

TABLE OF CONTENTS

Preface, xi

Acknowledgments, xv

Persistence	17
Duty	19
Desires of Our Hearts	22
Life	24
According to His Plans	26
Doubt	28
Ears to Hear	30
Jesus Saves	32
Know Your Word	34
On the Third Day	36
His Perfect Timing	38
He Restores My Soul	40
For Your Works	41
Broken-hearted	43
What People Think	45
Atoned	47
Rainbows	49
Love Thy Enemies	51
Do You Know Him?	53
Transform	55

- Who Am I Supposed to Be? 57
- You Are Not Alone 59
- Is Your Confidence in God? 61
- Forgive 63
- One Accord 65
- A New Thing 67
- Mary Did You Know? 69
- Hope 72
- Reward 75
- Fall in Love with Jesus 77
- Fruitful 79
- Shift 81
- He Never Knew You 83
- Worth the Wait 85
- God's Reflection 86
- Burn 88
- Rain 90
- Write It Down 92
- Not the Other Way Around 94
- Character vs. Reputation 96
- Who Can Be Against You? 98
- Jesus Wept 100
- Tumbleweeds 102
- Serve 104
- Provision 106
- Run Your Race 108

Not in Vain 110
Delay Is Not Denial 112
Live in Love 114
Give You Rest 116
No Strings Attached 118
So Close 121

PREFACE

When we think of God and our choice to follow Him, we often paint this picture of perfection. We assume that from the day we accept Christ as our Lord and Savior, everything will miraculously be fixed, and for the remainder of our lives, we'll be free of troubles, free of problems, and free of pain. Where did we ever get this idea that growth of any kind would be comfortable?

In 2 Corinthians 5:17, it says, "Therefore, if anyone is in Christ, he is a new creation old things have passed away; behold, all things have become new." Now, if you're reading this, it's safe to assume that you're over the age of 9 or 10, meaning you have, at this point, learned to walk, talk, eat, drink, and dress yourself. Well, according to THE WORD, and despite you learning these things before, the moment you give your life to the Lord, the ways that you've been doing these things are now considered old and passed away. In essence, you are starting all over again.

Now, from what I could see, learning to do these things the first time wasn't all that bad, but God has His reasons for wanting us to learn them again. When we initially learned how to walk, talk, eat, drink, and dress ourselves, we did so with the intent to merely survive. However, in being born again, God has us relearn these things with not just the intent of survival, but for the love of Christ and with the intent of purpose. Therefore, you are no longer walking just to walk; you are now walking in the righteousness of Jesus. You're no longer speaking empty words, but also speaking life into people. You don't crave foods like nachos and pizza, but instead, daily bread of the word. Your favorite drink isn't lemon water, but living water, and you're no longer pressed to be dressed in anything other than humility. But let's be honest, change like that doesn't just happen overnight.

Subsequently, we have to grow into these new beings, and there's nothing comfortable about growing. Trust me, I know. When I first started writing The Four Blue Walls, I had no idea that there were "new levels" to reach in my faith and that these new levels would be molding me, shaping me and changing me for the better. I was naive in my understanding of God. I thought that once I hopped aboard the Jesus train, my life would be spiritually on cruise control, but boy, was I in for a rude awakening.

As a matter of fact, in my prequel "One Psalm at a Time," I was so new in my faith that you could read and feel what I truly went through, expressing in my poems the basic ups and downs of what it means to be a believer and only knowing the basics. In another sense, I was writing from what I call a "level one" perspective. "The Four Blue Walls," however, was written from a level two standpoint and, in some parts, a level three perspective. In my childhood home, I spent 18 years of my life living in a room filled with baby blue walls. My fondest memories and deepest heartaches took place in that room. I gave my life to the Lord in that room. I wrote "One Psalm at a Time" in that room. I became every bit of the woman and warrior that I am today because of those "Four Blue Walls." What makes this sequel so special is that these are the last poems that I would ever have the pleasure of writing in that room.

Again, God has His way of doing things. I was crawling into my new relationship with Him in "One Psalm at a Time." However, as you begin to read part two of my writings in this book, you will find me walking, talking, eating, drinking, and dressing much differently than I did before truly maturing before your eyes because, I get it now. The presence of growth and pain is not the absence of God's love; it's an indicator of it. From the moment you accept Christ into your heart and deem Him Lord over your life, you are now a child, a "new creation" set out to endure the growing pains of spiritual life while fighting to complete your role in God's will.

Yes, growth is indeed uncomfortable, but it is so necessary for change, necessary for freedom, and most importantly, necessary for us to finally hear those words, "Well done my good and faithful servant" (Matthew 25:21). The journey here was no ordinary ride, but I pray that you walk away feeling just as encouraged, filled, and loved as I did in writing it. So, without further ado, welcome to "The Four Blue Walls."

Enjoy.

ACKNOWLEDGEMENTS

Writing and creating this book was really an eye-opening experience from start to finish. I learned a lot about myself, my worldview, the strength of my faith, and the lengths of my maturity. I essentially learned who God truly is and how His love and support are never ending. And that's exactly who I want to begin with. God, thank you for being who you are. Not one word of this book would be possible without you. I am grateful and humbled that you blessed me with this gift of poetry and honored that you trust me to share it with the world. Thank you for your only begotten son to whom I know and love as my Lord and Savior. Your sacrifice is the reason I write, the reason I live, and the reason I am who I am. And thank you for The Holy Spirit that dwells within me, who nudges me, encourages me and guides me every single day.

To my family, I thank you for continuously believing in me and pushing me to be the best poet, author and all-around artist that I can be. Your support means more than the world to me, and I know in the future we'll look back at this entire journey with the biggest smiles on our faces saying that every moment of it was worth it.

Next, I would like to thank my pastor and my church family at New Destiny Christian Ministries. For almost five years, you guys have cheered me on and allowed me to stand before you week after week to recite my poetry. Words alone cannot express how grateful I am for you all and how the opportunities that you guys have led me to over the years have changed my life. As a whole, you guys are proof of God's love, and I am blessed to be a part of such a caring and supportive church family.

And lastly, I would like to thank you, the reader, for your overall curiosity and interest in reading The Four Blue Walls. You holding this book right now brings more joy to my heart than you could imagine. You've truly helped to make one of my wildest dreams come true, and for that, with all sincerity, I thank you.

PERSISTENCE

There will be days
Where you'll be weary
There will be days
You will have to wait
There will be days
Where you'll feel nothing
And then some days
You can't concentrate

There will be weeks
With no improvement,
Disappointments
Will come left and right
Seeking guidance
You're hearing silence
And shedding tears
Every day and night

But no one said
It would be easy
Denying self
For your salvation
And loving Christ,
Who paid our price,
Comes with its trials

And tribulations

So please be strong
And be of good cheer
Live in pure peace
With no resistance
He's overcome
This turbulent world
And we'll make it
With persistence

DUTY

Your faith without
Works is nothing
Rome wasn't built
In just a day

Jesus took time to recruit
And aim in pursuit
And John the Baptist
Prepared the way

Moses had to
Climb that mountain
Noah really
Had to build that ark

David set out a plan
Then defeated a man
And as a boy
He left his mark

Peter had to
Follow instructions
Aaron always
Just knew what to say

Jonah delayed
But later obeyed
After his attempt
Of running away

Elijah spoke his truth,
And conquered evil
Elisha did double
But still the same

Jacob followed the Lord
And on one accord
Birthed a nation
From his name

See, our work
Has no exceptions
It's either done
Or not at all

We make the decision
As God grants us permission
We have that choice
To rise and even fall

We can succeed
If we put in the effort
It doesn't matter
That we are flawed

Duty is ours
And it's ours first
Then the results
Are up to God

DESIRES OF OUR HEARTS

We all have wants
For something greater
Than our current
Points of view

We have dreams of
Moving mountains
Replacing old
With something new

Jobs that really
Pay our worth
Instead of pennies
On the dime

Also, goals that
Go unspoken
And keep us broken
Half the time

Ideas and inventions
Books and even poems
Cars and vacations
Businesses and homes

Love with true commitment
Friends who really care
Kids who truly listen
Parents who are there

Oh Lord, hear our prayers
Aloud or in our heads
In the mornings as we rise
Or as we slumber in our beds

Provider of our needs from whom
Our purpose ends and starts
You know what we desire
And may you grant them to our hearts

Amara Kursha

LIFE

Life's about purpose
And mission
Life doesn't end
With a loss and death

Every day is a gift
And though it is swift
Please be thankful
For life and breath

Life was not meant
To be simple
Life was not meant
To be fair

But you can fulfill
Everything in His will
If you believe it
And if you so dare

Life is not defined
By others
Life is not defined
By our stuff

The fact that you're here
Just breathing in air
Is proof alone
That you are enough

Life is more than
Just a number
Life is more than
Just a line

And what we choose
To do in between
Can make a difference
In yours and mine

We're truly in this
Thing together
Linked by Jesus'
Life, way and light

And to show our thanks
We must keep Him first
And do our best
To live ours right

Amara Kursha

ACCORDING TO HIS PLANS

I wrote them out on tablets
Fully permanent and plain
I told Him all the things I planned
Yet our plans were not the same

What I wanted was really simple
Nothing hard and out of reach
No poetry, writing, art or songs
And not my pastor asking me to preach

What I desired was mediocre
Compared to all that was in store
And now I thank God I no longer desire
Those things I once wanted before

See, what we want and need are so different
And the difference is deeper than we think
So deep that the decision to follow His vision
Will determine if we float or if we sink

For He knows the plans He has for us
All the present, future and past
Like those people and things we wanted forever
But for whatever reason, they just couldn't last

Yes, everything happens for a reason
In its own season, place, and time
And those little ideas we think are big
Can't be compared to what He has in mind

I've learned it's best to surrender all
And to just leave it in His hands
Because the vision I had for my life
Was truly nothing according to His plans

DOUBT

Have you ever questioned
God and His motives
And wanted answers
When you had to grieve?

Lost sight of the good
That He's done in your life
And found every fault
In your faith to believe?

Have you ever seen
God do the impossible
Yet forget what you saw
Was in fact unique?

Then you go back to
Complaining, still stagnant
Remaining so poor
And spiritually weak

Oh, we of little faith
Must we constantly
See His many scars
And touch the holes

To know He's risen
And that He's living
In the center
Of our very souls

Are we Moses?
Are we Isaac?
Are we Thomas?
Are we Peter?

I know we are
Only human
But are we doubters
Or believers?

Yes, faith and doubt
Can't coexist
Just only one
Can be the key

And Jesus said
That blessed are those
Who still believe
But cannot see

EARS TO HEAR

We're all seeds
In heaven's garden
Scattered wide
To be sown

And in time
There will be judgment
Just to see
How we've grown

Truth is all
May never make it
Pass the hardness
Of the stones

Or proceed
Because the weeds
Choked the hunger
From their bones

And only some
Will ever see
From the heights
Of a tree

Planted in His
Perfect soil
Where Jesus toiled
For us to be

Yet just a few
Will get the message
Reaping blessings
From the root

Hearing God
And His truth
Reaching souls
Bearing Fruit

Amara Kursha

JESUS SAVES

Long before
We were believers
Word receivers
Spreading the news

We were scheming
World deceiving
Walking left in
Sinners shoes

Slowly dying
Testi-lying
Unaware of
Our behavior

On the brink
Of self-destruction
Oh, thank God
We have a Savior!

Heaven sent
With perfect purpose
Prince of Peace
His name is Jesus

Son of God
Son of Man
Sent to change
And to release us

He's the way
The truth, the life
The reason
We're no longer slaves

The Hero
Of our faith
Jesus lives
Jesus saves

KNOW YOUR WORD

There will surely
Come a time
This truth, I know
And you will see

You'll be questioned
About Jesus,
Who He is
And claims to be

With your faith
Now on the line
Will you arise
Or be deferred?

The answer's
In the question
Do you really
Know your word?

Bits and pieces
Here and there
Won't do the trick
For sinner souls

But chapter, verse
Self-immersed
Well-rehearsed
Can fill some holes

The more you know
And meditate
Can change the world
For them and me

Because someday
You will be
The only Bible
Some will see

ON THE THIRD DAY

They knew that
He was coming
Yes, a savior
Born to be

They wrote it
And they spoke it
On every scroll
And prophecy

A man who was
Beyond the normal
A great prophet
Who would heal

A servant
From a virgin
Sent to die
To close the deal

Yet when He came
They didn't notice
They were lost
In worshipping

Rules and laws
That left them blinded
Not open-minded
To see the King

So, at a cost
They gave the cross
To the man
They claimed had lied

Son of God
Living water
That was scourged,
Crowned and crucified

Left behind
A stone to rest
Forever gone
And locked away

So, they thought
When two days passed
But forever changed
On that third day

Amara Kursha

HIS PERFECT TIMING

Now I'll admit
I am a bit
Impatient
When I pray

Telling God
Just what I want
Needing answers
On that day

Disregarding
His procedures
Truth, book
And protocol

Forgetting who
Created whom
In my rush
To have it all

Not thinking
Just for a second
In the middle
Of my whining

He's orchestrating
Life and making right
My written path
And still aligning

Perfect pieces
Bits of better
People, places
Things to be

Plans of future
Pleasant blessings
Way beyond that
I could see

But eventually
I have learned
You must not rush
Your own refining

Because faith
Grows while we wait
On His great
And perfect timing

Amara Kursha

HE RESTORES MY SOUL

When all the world is dreary
When all my skies are gray
When pain has me stuck
And life has me struck
Speechless with none to say

When night turns to mourning
And morning just a day
The only one to clear the hurt
Is Jesus, He's the life
The truth and the way

His power guides the lost
His mighty strength
Fully makes us better
His truth sets us free
And His love endures forever

Darkness may surround me
But I know who's in control
Hope is in my heart
And through my heart
He restores my soul

FOR YOUR WORKS

Some say the best things
In this life are free
Zero down without a price
And I say, just the opposite
I truly believe that
All things come with sacrifice

You must be willing
To be much better
So determined to succeed
More than ready to be used
And well prepared
To sweat and bleed

You must follow
Your given Instructions
Quick without delay
Trust with your heart
And not your eyes
Then consciously obey

Fight your mighty flesh
Resist the world
And wrestle sin
Faith it 'til you make it

And love the Lord
That lives within

Then is when you'll see
That nothing is free
And your efforts are supported
Please just stay strong
And be courageous
For your work shall be rewarded

BROKEN-HEARTED

Pain is proof
That you're living
But it's unforgiving
With its aim

Straight for
The heart
It leaves a mark
Without a stain

Attacking
Every feeling
Then revealing
Shattered hope

And leaving you
Searching for some light
To make it right
And ways to cope

But in the darkness
You would find
That in your bind
You're not alone

Amara Kursha

Among the shadows
Of your grief
Stands our chief
The cornerstone

Wholly ready
To amend
And restore
What's departed

Saving souls
Sealing holes
And truly healing
The broken-hearted

WHAT PEOPLE THINK

There will always
Be someone judging
No matter the bad
Or the good that you do

You could share with society
Your whole wide world
And still they'd ask you
To see Saturn too

Your name's not
Exempt from gossip
Strangely, strangers
Would have things to say

You could do everything right
Yet, just to break you down
People would do the most
And go out of their way

But don't you dare
Forget that you're special
Remember it is He
Who lives in your soul

Amara Kursha

Not these wicked people
Tearing you to pieces
Day by day to make
Themselves look whole

And it's not your job
To please them
Because this life
Is but a blink

Stay true to yourself
Be no one else
Because who cares
What people think.

ATONED

My mistakes,
Come by the thousands
My wrongs,
outweigh my rights

My faults shine brighter
Than the stars above
As my sins
Grow taller in heights

You would think that
I'm destined for failure
And my good deeds are
Few and far between

But what if I said
I was saved
By the blood of a Man
And was made so clean

Then my mistakes
Would have no meaning
Then my wrongs
Couldn't bring me down

Amara Kursha

My faults would be
Just a speck in the sky
While my sins would grow
Hope from the ground

For God wouldn't see me standing
Alone with the things I have done
He would see perfection and righteousness
Through the stains and blood of His Son

So now I live in peace from knowing
I need not fear death or being stoned
Because Jesus laid down His life for me
And through His love I was fully atoned.

RAINBOWS

He warned me
Of the storms in life
And constantly
They're brewing

And though the clouds
Are coming
They can't stop
What I've been doing

I built my ark
Upon His word
I'm protected
Through this pain

He prepared me
Through my tears
So, I don't flinch
When I see rain

Tribulation
Is a given
Trials and troubles
Are guaranteed

Amara Kursha

I may not get
Just what I want,
But He will give me
Just what I need

And these storms
Don't last forever
That one truth
I surely know

I'm strong and loved
The proof is found
In the presence
Of every rainbow.

LOVE THY ENEMIES

There will be those
Who persecute you
And others that will
Slander your name

Some will fake their love
And support for you
Then they'll recant
Like life is a game

People will lie
And loudly judge you
Fools will use you
Until they're done

Some bullies will
Tear your life apart
And carry on
As if they've won

And for a moment
It may look like
They're above you
And sadly, you're beneath

Amara Kursha

You were fearfully
And wonderfully made
By God out of love
And not defeat

Yes, the pain may hurt
But you're not at fault
For their ignorance
And blindness

And the remedies
For these enemies
Is to fully kill
Their hate with kindness

So, love thy neighbor
As commanded
And love thy God
With all you do

Then fight to forgive
Both them and you
And learn to love
Thy enemies too

DO YOU KNOW HIM?

Tell me, which one came first
The blessing or the praise?
You would know if you knew Him more
Than once a week and holidays

If you called Him at this moment
Would He answer like a friend?
Or would your number be unknown
And be unanswered 'til the end?

Do you know His famous story
Often spoken, yet denied?
Born unprivileged in a manger
Then was whipped and crucified?

Do you know His in between
Healing the sick and raising the dead?
Do you know His written word
Both prophesied and inked in red?

Do you know His friends and family
And with the Father He is one?
And when He rose up on that third day
New life was soon to come?

Amara Kursha

Do you know that in His name
He's conquered earth and even hell?
Well, judging by your actions
If you said you knew Him, I couldn't tell.

TRANSFORM

We weren't called
To be still and stagnant
We were chosen to
Change and grow.

The 'you' that you see,
That wants to be free
Should be the 'you'
That you used to know.

Don't applaud
What you did yesterday
For today is a
Different frame.

And through the lens of life
When the picture's right
You should develop
And not be the same.

Who you are
In this very moment
You need not be
When it's time to leave.

Amara Kursha

For our God
Makes you anew
Deep down in your heart
If you choose to believe.

He sent His word
In human flesh
To save, to warn
And to inform.

And from His blood
We ought to learn
To love, to stretch
And to transform.

WHO AM I SUPPOSED TO BE?

Who am I supposed to be?
These doubts in my head
Are really screaming
I saw a glimpse
Of what you said
But maybe I was dreaming

My eyes are closed
The road is black
This path I cannot see
These future plans
That's in your hands,
That you mapped out for me

Lord, this is your life
This is your will
But I want success
I tried to do it
All on my own
That, you wouldn't bless

So, now I guess
The secret lies within
My patience and my trust
To wait on you

And to listen clearly
For instructions, then adjust

Because what others have
Is not meant for me
Our purposes aren't the same
Yes, I see it now
It is all for good
And you were not to blame

The truth is simple
Just keep You first
Obedience is key
And then that is when
I'll soon begin to see
Who I'm supposed to be.

YOU ARE NOT ALONE

That feeling of exclusion
Thinking, no one will understand
It's only you that's going through this
Yes, this problem that's at hand

Almost eight billion other people
Live and occupy this earth
But in your mind, you've told yourself
That you're the only one feeling hurt

You think your problems are 'your' problems
And there's no purpose in the mix
But, in fact, you hold the answer
For another soul to get a fix

We go through trials and tribulations
To speak truth and testify
In every crowd there'll be a person
That can too identify

With your truth, they'll see themselves
And in your story, there's a 'we'
That's why it's crucial to keep fighting
For as you fight, you're saving 'me'

Me, the person in the crowd
Feeling lost and on my own
Now I know I'm not the only one
Thank God, I'm not alone.

IS YOUR CONFIDENCE IN GOD?

I think it often slips our minds
He's awesome, our creator
Of all the earth and skies above
Do you know there's no one greater?

But in time when life begins to test
Our faith, we fold and nod
Rejecting what we know is true
So, is your confidence in God?

When you're stressed and feel oppressed
By the trials that have you bound
Do you trust that He will halt your pain
And have you walking on dry ground?

Are your thoughts of Him so limited
You look to man for your Amen?
And do you believe He can wire the mouths
Of your haters as you're sitting in the lion's den?

You must know that your God is strong
All powerful, almighty and precise
Do you see He'd move heaven and earth
Without ever thinking twice?

Amara Kursha

His heart is pure and His touch real,
His abounding love never stops
So, the answer lies in whether or not
'You' choose to put Him in a box.

FORGIVE

Is that thing you said you're over
Really over in your mind?
Does it hurt to see them move along
When you gave them all your time?

Do those memories come flashing
Setting fire to your soul
Burning deep just like their lies
When your side was never told?

Does the mention of their name
Make you shift in your position?
If they failed would you applaud
As though your pain was competition?

Do you sit and ever wonder
Did this person ever care?
Did you struggle needing help
And found that person wasn't there?

'It isn't fair,' is what you're thinking
And I'm here to say, 'it's true'
Can you imagine what you think of them
Someone else may think of you?

Amara Kursha

All to God, has fallen short
Of what it means to truly live
So, you'll find freedom and God's favor
In your choice to soon forgive.

ONE ACCORD

We see through many lenses
On everything we won't agree
And division is a threat
To all of which we've grown to be.

The body is a unit
The church is who we are
Disciples of His Word
Hearts and souls near and far.

Sinners all alike
We're all evil at the core
Just reaching for the light
Really wanting to be more.

Love is our commandment
And together we must work
Hash it out from head to toe
Though no matter how it hurts.

Bind and be a group
And create some organization
Despite our chosen rules
Governed by denomination.

Jesus is the reason
It's time to climb aboard
Throw out our silly differences
And live all on one accord.

A NEW THING

No more looking back
On yesterday
For today is
A new beginning

In the past
You may have lost
But at God's cost
You'll soon be winning

Memories
Of your enemies
Will fade like darkness
In the dawn

And that feeling
To be appealing
To the world
Will too be gone

The word "old"
Will not uphold
Within your spirit
For it's anew

Amara Kursha

You won't find pleasure
None whatsoever
In those things
You used to do

Remember not
Your former self
Because before you
Stands "The King"

And from your sins
New life begins
Because through Him
You are a new thing

MARY, DID YOU KNOW?

Mary, Did You Know
That in that moment
Your womb would glow
Marking the start
Of this conception
Forever changing
Your perception?

Did it ever cross
Your mind
That this son
Would be divine,
Mending the sick
And healing the blind
Turning water into wine?

Could you even
Comprehend
That He's the one that
God would send
The Alpha and Omega
The beginning
And the end?

When you heard

Amara Kursha

His name was Jesus
Did your heart
Leap and quiver
For this child that you would
Birth had come to earth
To soon deliver?

Did you feel it
In your soul
That this child
Would make you whole
Fulfilling every prophecy
Written then
On every scroll?

Did the truth reveal itself
Or did you see a true
Connection
That He would die
So we could live
Through His love and
Resurrection?

When you first

Held Him close
Was it then you realized
Of all the babies
In the world
You were looking God
In His eyes?

Mary, Did You Know?

HOPE

Hope is the driving force
That's keeping us sane
It's hard to explain
But you can't have faith
Without hope
It's like trying to breathe
With no lungs or throwing
Anchors with no rope.

See, hope led Moses
To the promise land
Of milk and honey
Through seas divided
It saved Isaac
On that mountain high
And through its power
God provided.

It even helped Job
To overcome
Satan's plot
Of death and pain
It helped Noah
Build that
Wooden ark

Without ever seeing rain.

Because hope is
More than wishing,
Hope is
Solid in its truth
Hope gave
Abram many nations
Hope brought
Boaz to his Ruth.

Hope drove
Saul to repentance
John had hope
In what he said
Hope lead
David to his victory
Hope rose
Jesus from the dead.

Hope is
More than just a want,
Hope is
Knowing that it's done,

Hope is
Feeling like you're
Losing
But believing you've won.

Hope is
Real if you have it
It's a key
To our salvation
Hope is
The good and the glue
To our
Spiritual foundation.

REWARD

If money is what
You're after
Sad to say
You've been mistaken.

It's not worth
The time that's ticking
Nor that back
That you've been breaking

If it's fame
You really seek
And this attention
You desire

There's no value
In a 'title'
That could never
Take you higher

If it's things
You have to have
And they're a need
In your perception

I hope you want
For something more
Before you fall
For their deception

In this life
There will be work
Both for self
And for the Lord

And for whom
You work the hardest
Will determine
Your reward.

FALL IN LOVE WITH JESUS

There is nothing like
Your first love
Heart beating
Out your chest
Your knees weak
From emotion
They were nothing
Like the rest

You would study
Their behavior
Lose track of
All your time
Hanging on to
Every word
And they were
Always on your mind

And I say the same
For Jesus
He's much greater
Than your first
Because He loves you
At your best
And most importantly

At your worst

You would study
His behavior
And be wiser
With your time
Then digest
His every word
And be renewed
Soul and mind

Unlike your first
He'd never hurt you
He put you first
Above it all
So, I think it's time
You fell in love
Knowing that
Jesus is worth the fall

FRUITFUL

Every tree
And every man
From every top
And every root

Will be known
By how it lives
Standing bare
Or bearing fruit

And the outcome
Is a matter
Of their choices
Rooted deep

If they sway
From good to bad
And by the company
They keep

If they wither
In the weather
Or give in
To what's around

Amara Kursha

They won't be reaching
For the heavens
But be falling
Toward the ground

There's no good
In having nothing
Ask yourself
And just be truthful

In the works
You have provided
Are you bare
Or are you fruitful?

SHIFT

Time is what
You're wasting
If you choose
To never change

Those goals and dreams
That you have written
Will forever remain
Out of your range

If your habits
Stay the same
Who's to blame
For no success?

If your spirit's
Not maturing
Can you really
Live your best?

If your mind
Is not increasing
And your learning
Is at a halt

Don't be saddened
By the truth
When you're living
At a fault.

The race will not
Be given to
The strong, the smart
And the swift

But to the souls
That move with God
And then respond
And choose to shift.

HE NEVER KNEW YOU

You actually ran
And told the world
It's in your heart
That you believe

But in the dark
Where you live your life
It's them and self
That you deceive

Yes, be foolish
If you'd like
Sin in peace
And live in youth

But don't you give
This world your love
And say you claim
To know the truth

For your lies
Will be displayed,
Judgement made
And then you'll see

Amara Kursha

This life was more
Than your fulfillment
And being that saint
You claimed to be

So, in that moment
At the gate
It's there you'll wait
For how He'll view

And if you choose
To never change
He will say, in fact
He never knew you

WORTH THE WAIT

Always anxious for an answer
Surely suffering in worry
I did this when I prayed
And didn't see blessings in a hurry

But worrying got me nowhere
I was suffering in vain
Because patience is a virtue
And it doesn't have to equal pain

I was truly growing stronger
As the days and weeks went by
Trusting God knew what I needed
And in time He would supply

Everything my heart requested
Just as long as they aligned
With His will and the desires
That He had for me in mind

And when the moment would arrive
No other feeling could equate
To the joy and appreciation
Making it all just worth the wait

Amara Kursha

GOD'S REFLECTION

My mirror
Once was broken,
And its image
Was distorted.

Who I was
And what I saw,
Based on His Word
Were not supported.

When I walked
Into a room,
I always questioned
What they see.

Was it God
In all His glory,
Or the sinner
Known as 'me'?

So, I gathered
All my pieces,
And just laid them
At His feet.

I watched Him
Change my life,
And mend my heart
To be complete.

Now, I look
Into my mirror,
With no faults
Or imperfection.

For the image
Staring back,
Is not myself
But God's reflection.

BURN

Faith is like a fire
Full of power
When contained.

Placed in every heart
With the potential, a desire
To be tamed.

If it's misused
Some will suffer, left confused
And all misled.

If it's abused
Hate will rise, and then the
Innocent be dead.

If it's controlled
More would seek it, for its warmth
And its light.

If it's shared
With good intention, it could change
Wrong to right.

A simple spark

With major purpose, from its strength
We can learn.

So, If you fuel
Your faith with love, the world will come
Watch it burn.

RAIN

Am I a symbol of misfortune
Or a blessing in disguise?

Depends on your perception
When you look up to the skies.

Are you living in a season
Where your drought is getting wider?

And you assumed you were the source,
But now need help from the provider?

Are you drowning in your sins
Where pain and pleasure are your friends?

And are you trying to play it off,
When, in fact, you want a cleanse?

Are you waiting for a sign
That it's now time for you to grow?

And you're clinging to the past,
When you need to let it go?

See, the power I possess

Is well beyond what you could know.

I quench and clean and in between
Help to reap what others sow.

I may ruin some parades
And escapades so you'll complain.

But I'm an answer to the prayers
Of those who want His love to rain.

WRITE IT DOWN

A goal is just a wish
Until it's inked upon a page,
And your will to make it happen
Is the tone that sets the stage.

If you wait until you're 'ready'
Just beware, you'll never be
So save yourself the time and trouble
Way before the 'woe is me'.

No one else can do your work
Which is required to succeed
And you will sit just where you are
Until that want becomes a need.

Good intentions, get you nothing
And potential, no reward
You neglecting to do more
Is not something you can afford.

There may not be another chance,
Another now, another way
All you have is just this moment
And all you need is just today.

Don't take for granted your location
And the gifts that you've been given
Don't just say what you desire
Without a map to do the mission.

God has blessed you with a vision
There's no time to play around
You're much closer than you think
You just have to write it down.

NOT THE OTHER WAY AROUND

In this world, we've painted a picture
Of what we want our God to be
Loving, faithful, fully passive
And unable to disagree.

He could give us His suggestions
But in this life, we'll be the guide
No more praying, just disobeying
And we still expect Him to provide.

Full acceptance of our choices
Into the gates we'll enter in
There will be no more falling short
And no more penalty for sin.

We want a God to give us plenty
And to ignore Him with our soul
Until we need Him for a problem
We want a God we can control.

Yet we've painted this twisted picture
With our fully human hands
Both imperfect and incapable
To change God and all His plans.

He's the same, as He was before
And no matter what we try to do
We can't shrink Him down to size
To make Him look like me and you.

So we need to fix our vision
And see who truly wears the crown
Because He made us in His image
Not the other way around.

CHARACTER VS. REPUTATION

Who you are
When no one's looking
Matters more
Than what they see

You could fake it
For the world
But be just like
The enemy

Full of hate
In one direction
Full of love
In yet another

Fooling everyone
But God
Who knows the true you
From the other

Living life
As an undercover
Holy saint
That's doing right

Blind to see what you've
Done in the dark
Will soon be brought out
Into the light

And in the end
They'd see your character
All that is true
Without manipulation

And they would find
They fell for nothing
But the facade
Of your reputation

WHO CAN BE AGAINST YOU?

Defeat is just another lie
The devil places in your head
Snatching joy like Monday mornings
All before you leave your bed.

Don't give in to what he said
Have you thinking that he's won
Have you thinking that's it over
When this day has just begun.

He's the accuser, not the Son
So his words can hold no weight
Next to the truth that's inked in blood
Wiping the sins from every slate.

His plot and ploys aren't up for debate
For there's no power at their core
He simply starts these mini battles
Because he cannot win the war.

Your victory's is yet in store
Because the Father's on your side
Blocking the blows from your flesh
And all the tricks the enemy tried.

It's protection God provides
And every promise guaranteed
So you can greet this day with hope
Knowing you have just what you need.

Yes, you're covered and you're freed
His grace and love are your defense too
So when it's all said and done
Tell me who can be against you?

Amara Kursha

JESUS WEPT

If you're looking for a friend
And someone real to understand
The struggles that you're facing
Making it hard to even stand.

I assure you, right before you
If it's your faith that does not waiver
You will find within your reach
So ready to help is your Lord and Savior.

With open arms and so accepting,
You can show Him your frustration
For He knows your every pain
Yes, from the rejection to temptation.

Even more, if your funds are poor
And you find yourself just feeling lonely
Truly tired from this fight
I know He'd say, "You're not the only!"

He stood once where you're standing
Feeling hurt and seeing loss
Disappointed by those He loves
And all before He bore the cross

So, yet again, if you need a friend
Call on who walked where you have stepped
For He knows the help you need
And for your sorrows, He has wept.

TUMBLEWEEDS

Drifting on the surface
Only purpose to exist
No roots, forever thirsty
And by their nature, they resist

Refusing to be firm
So they turn from their foundation
And at the slightest hint of change
They're ready to go into rotation

Back and forth, South to North
Through the world and tossed around
While forgetting how it felt to be
Once planted in the ground

But they know better, yet the weather
Sets their path not God intended
And if confronted with His truth
You'll find their pride will be offended

Left to right, taking flight
Forging freedom as they roam
Making it seem their way is worth it
When they wish they could be home

No provision, lacking vision
Setting sail without a guide
Flowing helpless in the wind
Without a voice to so decide

They must suspend and put to an end
The spreading of their seeds
Because they walk among the church
And we don't need more tumbleweeds

SERVE

Can you call yourself a servant
If your faith is unemployed
Waiting fully for directions
But its signs you still avoid?

Can you say that He's your savior
In your heart that you believe
But when it comes to loving more
You cannot give but can receive?

Can you be one of the chosen
Knowing the laborers are few
Still living your life in sin
And have Him put His trust in you?

You should know your choices matter
And the consequence you cannot curve
So don't think your life is yours
And just do everything but serve.

If you do you miss your blessings
Both in heaven and on earth
Putting a limit on your God
Who wanted to give you what you're worth.

Don't you settle for this world
With all of its lies that look like perks
You may be walking by your faith
But now He wants to see your works.

PROVISION

God is higher
Than the boss
That is assigned
To sign your checks

So much bigger
Than the bank
That has no interest
But collects

He's more thoughtful
Than a lender
That only gives
To watch it earn

He's willing to fund
Your every dream
Only wanting
One thing in return

That you have faith
To trust His word
And faith in Him
To help you live

You must know
That it's His money
And from His money
He chooses to give

He gave you hope
Plans and a future
All to match
Your working vision

So believe that
He's got your back
And He will grant
You that provision

RUN YOUR RACE

You were sent here
On an assignment
With a purpose
To fulfill.

It's unique
To only you
To rightly fit
His perfect will.

Your techniques
Gifts and talents
Are all yours
With no mistake.

So don't look on
To others' blessings
Say theirs are real
And yours are fake.

Nothing's wrong
With your position
Just look forward
You're on track.

And there's no one
That can stop you
Only you can
Hold you back.

So keep fighting
And keep pushing
God will guide you
To first place.

The only way
That you will make it
Is if you stay
And run your race!

NOT IN VAIN

That work that you've been doing
Will produce its own reward
And those problems you've been facing
God has seen and not ignored.

All mistakes have been forgiven
They're so essential to the plan
You may not see it in the moment
But one day you'll understand.

Every second is a blessing
Not one gone has been unused
And there is a purpose in every time
You've been rejected and refused.

Just hold on a little longer
Don't give in to every trial
Because the cost to make it through
I know is surely worth your while.

There is meaning in your mourning
And a count for every tear
Plus the answers you've been seeking
Are not far but almost here.

So that loss was not a loss
But just a set up for your gain
I'm sorry that it hurt you
But please know it's not in vain.

DELAY IS NOT DENIAL

Let me guess,
That thing you asked for
Was not at all
You expected

In your soul
You know the truth
But still you're standing
Here dejected

How can answers
To your prayers
Be presented
In this way?

How can God
Just say keep going
But put your promotion
On delay?

'Does He hear me
When I pray?'
Is the question
You possess

Not ever thinking
That your timing
Is not His timing
At its best

So be humble
And be blessed
His love's enough
To make you wait

To testify
Your every truth
And praise His name
To make it great

And when it's done
You'll call it fate
Saying the pain
Was worth the ride

And some things
May be delayed
But that does not mean
They'll be denied

Amara Kursha

LIVE IN LOVE

Have you ever
Shown compassion,
Put a smile on
Someone's face,
Or went out of your way
Knowing they couldn't repay
And restored their faith
In the human race?

Can the homeless
Call your number?
Do the hungry
Know your name?
If the roles were reversed,
You were hungry and thirsty,
Would you want them
To treat you the same?

Can the young
Get your advice?
Can the old
Call you a friend?
Is your focus on yourself,
Needs, wants and wealth
That on your hand

People cannot depend?

The answer is in how
You treat others
Sisters and brothers
All around
So if all the world
Were searching
For your love
Could it be found?

We need each other
More than ever
And we're commanded
From above
To have faith
To walk in hope
But most of all
To live in love.

Amara Kursha

GIVE YOU REST

It's been yet
Another day
Another storm
Another test

And it seems that
Through your working
What's not working
Is your best.

It could be worse
Missing a roof
Lacking clothes
Food and a table

But that doesn't
Stop the grief
Yet you know
Your God is able.

Turn your trials
Into a triumph
Turn your pain
Into a praise

Turn your failure
Into renewed faith
Because His ways
Are not our ways.

So when the battle
Leaves you broken
And shattered
Lying in a mess

Draw unto Him
And you'll be blessed
Go to Him now
He'll give you rest.

Amara Kursha

NO STRINGS ATTACHED

If you asked God
If He loved you
How do you think
He would reply?

Would He speak light
Into the darkness
And put the heavens
Into the sky?

Would He birth you
In His image
Then proclaim you
As His own?

Would He be your pillar
Day and night
And to you say,
"You're not alone"?

Would He beg you
To obey Him
And work to show you
What is right?

Would He test you
Every season
And protect you
Through the fight?

Would He send
His only son
Knowing that
All you do is sin?

Would He clear you
Of your charges
If you choose to
Live for Him?

Well, His answer
Is in His actions
Only the truth
With no condition.

Unlike this crazy
World around you
For in their hearts
They would petition.

Amara Kursha

But your God
His love is unique
Despite your wrongs
Its strength unmatched.

He loves you
Through whatever
Your price was paid
No strings attached.

SO CLOSE

My breakthrough is on a flight
And it'll be landing very soon
There's no time for a delay
So for these plans I've made some room

I threw my past into the garbage
And flushed my pride into the sea
Rearranged my thoughts and faith
Then cleared my heart that's beating free

It doesn't need me to be perfect
But it needs me to be changed
So when it comes, I can't be hopeless
Looking foolish and deranged

I'm not allowed to be the same
It only travels where there's growth
I have the faith and done the work
It's only active when there's both

Yes, my time is truly coming
Thank you, God, for I'm now prepared
You helped me make it through this fight
So for this chapter, I'm not scared

Amara Kursha

I can see it in the distance
Gliding faster toward the coast
I may not have it right this second
But I know that it is close

www.ingramcontent.com/pod-product-compliance
Lightning Source LLC
Chambersburg PA
CBHW050436010526
44118CB00013B/1560